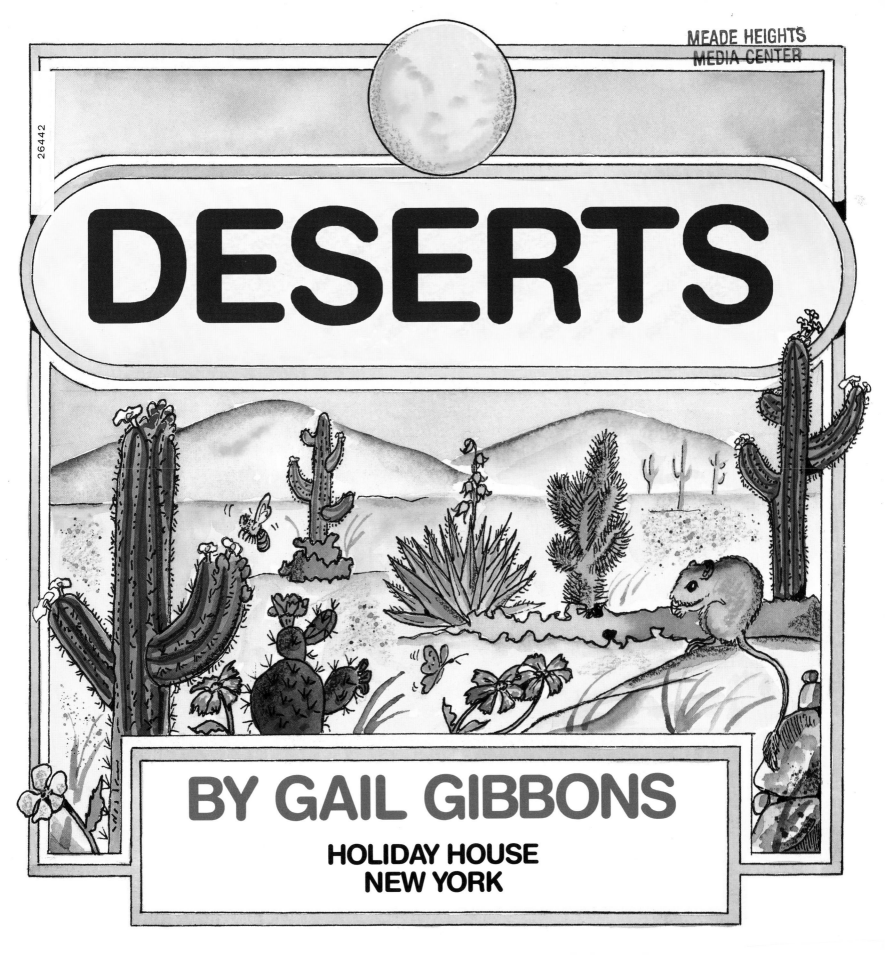

DESERTS

BY GAIL GIBBONS

HOLIDAY HOUSE
NEW YORK

Special thanks to Carol Cochran,
Director of Education and Programs, at
The Arizona Sonora Desert Museum,
Tucson, Arizona.

Library of Congress Cataloging-in-Publication Data
Gibbons, Gail.
    Deserts / by Gail Gibbons. — 1st ed.
    p.   cm.
    Summary: An introduction to the characteristics of deserts and the
plants and animals that inhabit them.
    ISBN 0-8234-1276-8 (hardcover : alk. paper)
    1. Deserts—Juvenile literature.   [1. Deserts.]   I. Title
GB612.G53   1996   96-4086   CIP   AC
508.315′4—dc20

To Tere LoPrete

All plants and animals in this book appear in North America;
exceptions are the Inland Taipan snake (Australia), the fennec
fox and golden wheel spider (Africa), and camels (Central
Asia, Africa, and the Middle East).

Dry ground, bright sunshine. It is hot and the sky is clear. It is daytime on the desert. A desert is a place that is very dry. In most deserts it rains less than ten inches a year.

SOME DESERTS OF THE WORLD

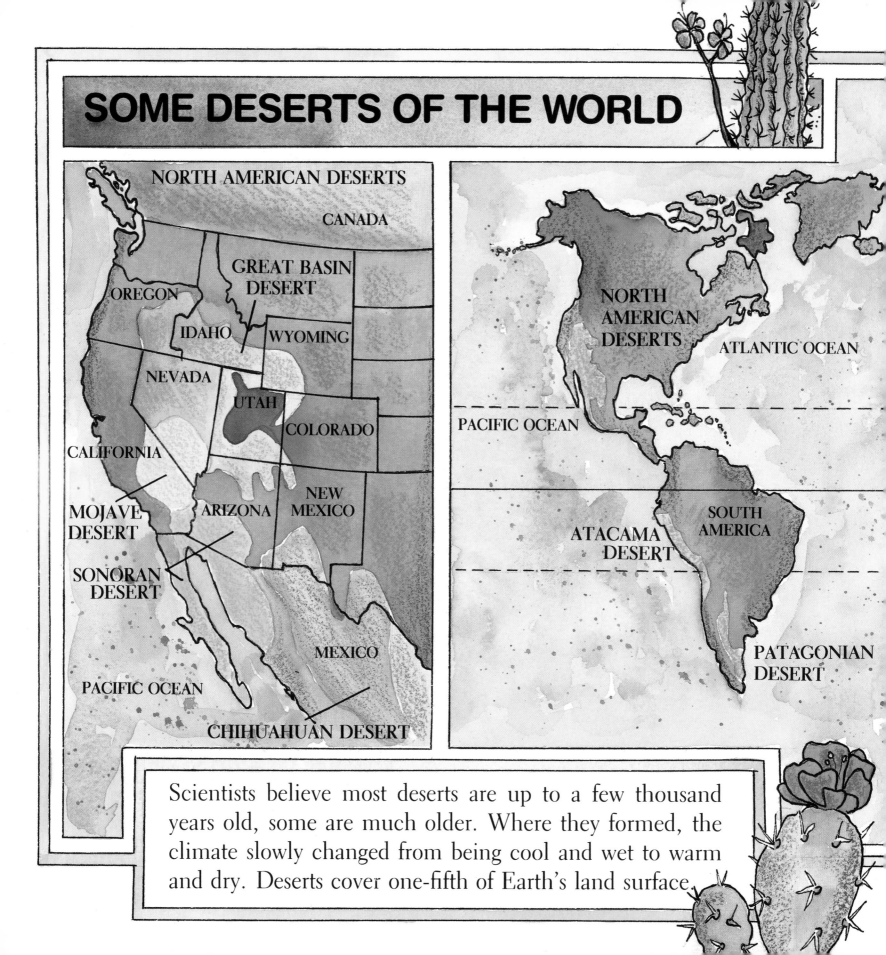

NORTH AMERICAN DESERTS

CANADA

GREAT BASIN DESERT

OREGON

IDAHO

WYOMING

NEVADA

UTAH

COLORADO

CALIFORNIA

MOJAVE DESERT

ARIZONA

NEW MEXICO

SONORAN DESERT

MEXICO

PACIFIC OCEAN

CHIHUAHUAN DESERT

NORTH AMERICAN DESERTS

ATLANTIC OCEAN

PACIFIC OCEAN

ATACAMA DESERT

SOUTH AMERICA

PATAGONIAN DESERT

Scientists believe most deserts are up to a few thousand years old, some are much older. Where they formed, the climate slowly changed from being cool and wet to warm and dry. Deserts cover one-fifth of Earth's land surface.

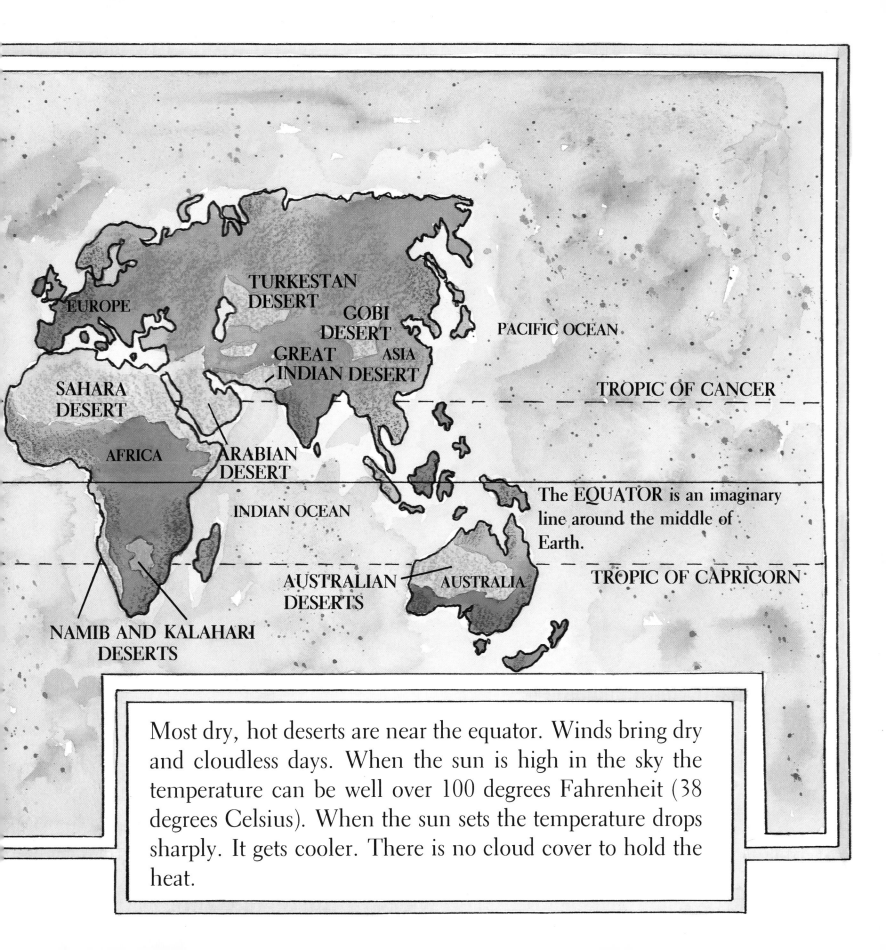

TURKESTAN
DESERT

EUROPE

GOBI
DESERT

PACIFIC OCEAN

GREAT
INDIAN DESERT

ASIA

SAHARA
DESERT

TROPIC OF CANCER

AFRICA

ARABIAN
DESERT

The EQUATOR is an imaginary
line around the middle of
Earth.

INDIAN OCEAN

AUSTRALIAN
DESERTS

AUSTRALIA

TROPIC OF CAPRICORN

NAMIB AND KALAHARI
DESERTS

Most dry, hot deserts are near the equator. Winds bring dry
and cloudless days. When the sun is high in the sky the
temperature can be well over 100 degrees Fahrenheit (38
degrees Celsius). When the sun sets the temperature drops
sharply. It gets cooler. There is no cloud cover to hold the
heat.

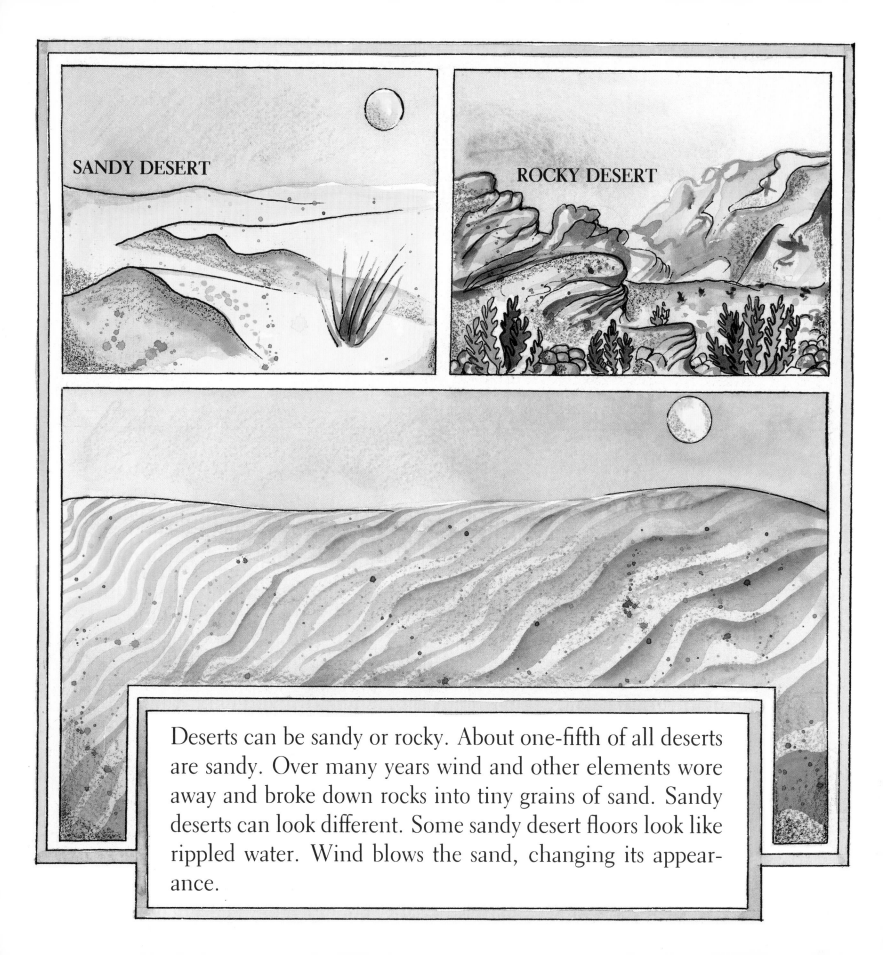

SANDY DESERT

ROCKY DESERT

Deserts can be sandy or rocky. About one-fifth of all deserts are sandy. Over many years wind and other elements wore away and broke down rocks into tiny grains of sand. Sandy deserts can look different. Some sandy desert floors look like rippled water. Wind blows the sand, changing its appearance.

DUNE

Others look uneven and lumpy. If something is in the sand's way, sand piles up behind it. On some sandy deserts strong winds blow the sand into smooth hills called dunes. Over time dunes can move.

Rocky deserts can look different and very strange. Often wind-blown sand wears rocks into odd shapes. Many deserts have jagged rocks. Sudden rains along with heat and cold crack the rocks and pieces break away.

Water EVAPORATES into the air.

Often the rain falls hard and fast. It runs off and sinks into the ground or evaporates.

Few plants and animals can live in the desert because it is so dry and hot. The ones that do live there have adapted to living without much water.

ORGAN PIPE CACTUS

SAGUARO CACTUS

STEM

BARREL CACTUS

LEAVES

CENTURY PLANT

ROOT

Many plants that live in the desert are called succulents. They take rainwater up through their roots to store in their leaves or stems for use during dry, hot spells.

PRICKLY PEAR CACTUS

BARREL CACTUS

PLEAT

HEDGEHOG
CACTUS

MEXICAN POPPY

A cactus is a succulent desert plant. The waxy surface on the stem helps keep in its water. Some have pleats that allow the cactus to expand with water when it rains. The cactus puffs up and the pleats almost disappear. As it uses up its water, the pleats become more visible again.

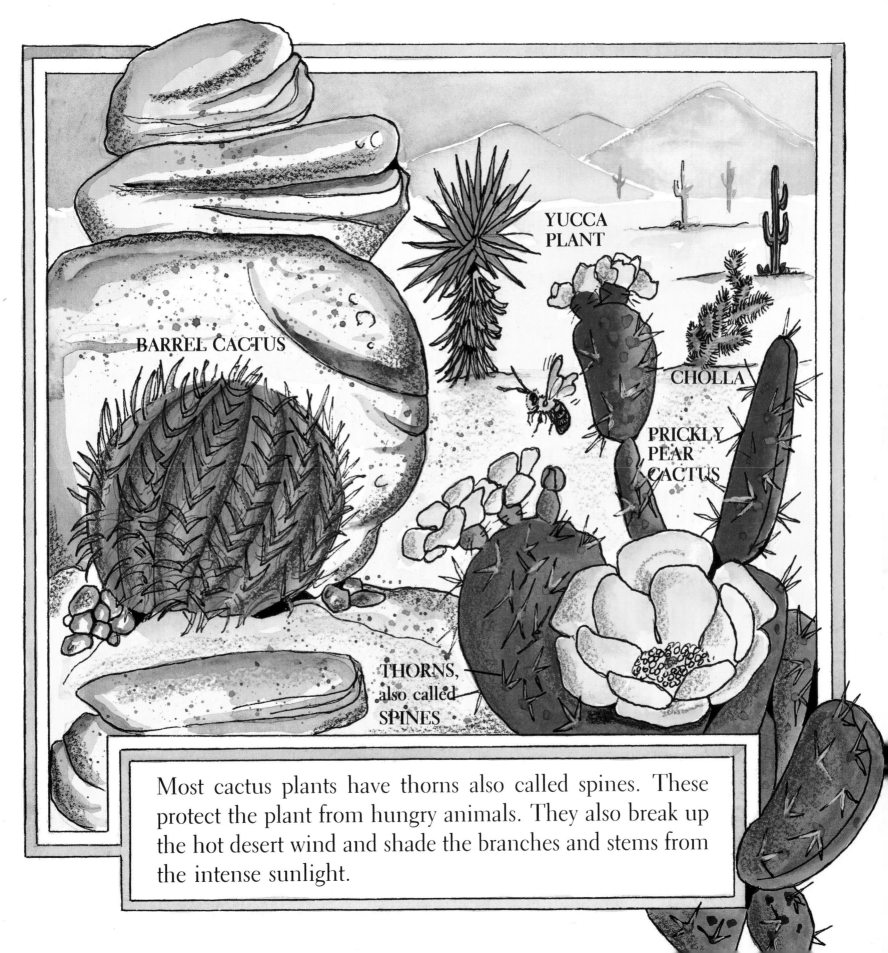

YUCCA PLANT

BARREL CACTUS

CHOLLA

PRICKLY PEAR CACTUS

THORNS, also called SPINES

Most cactus plants have thorns also called spines. These protect the plant from hungry animals. They also break up the hot desert wind and shade the branches and stems from the intense sunlight.

SAGUARO CACTUS

MESQUITE

TAPROOT

SHALLOW ROOTS

Desert plants need to get as much water as possible to survive. Some grow deep taproots. Sometimes these roots go down over one hundred feet to get to water. Others grow shallow roots that spread out to quickly absorb water from the lightest rainfall.

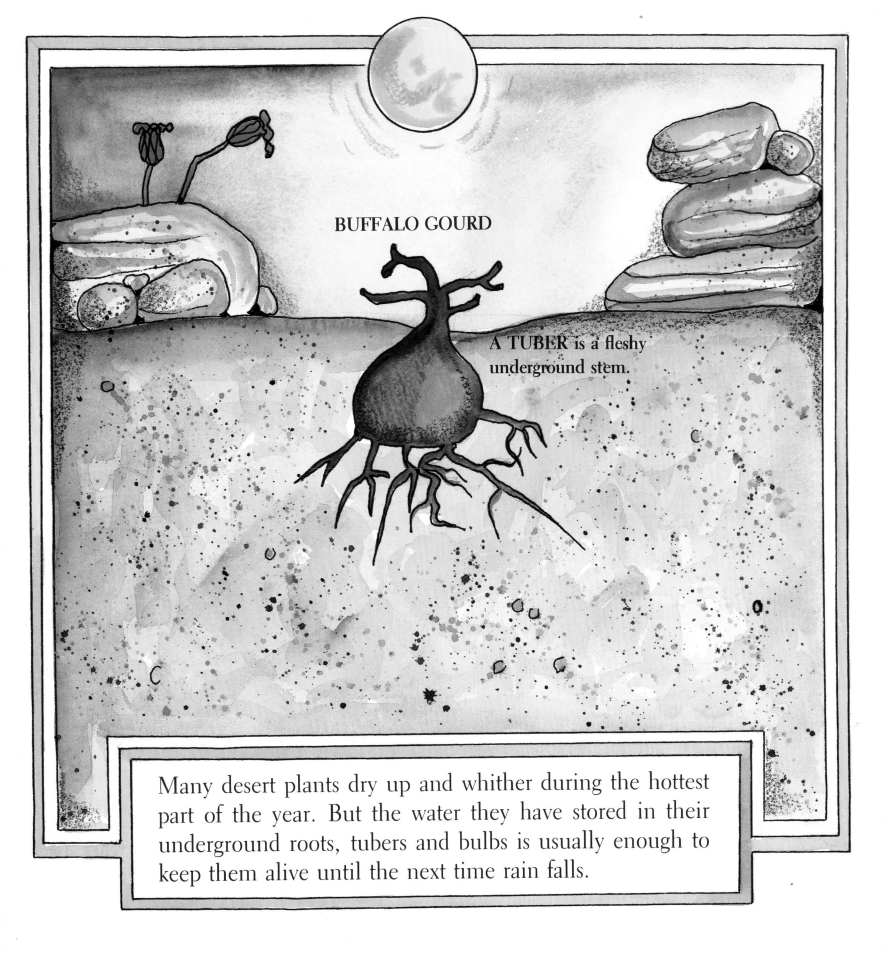

BUFFALO GOURD

A TUBER is a fleshy underground stem.

Many desert plants dry up and whither during the hottest part of the year. But the water they have stored in their underground roots, tubers and bulbs is usually enough to keep them alive until the next time rain falls.

In some deserts when it finally does rain, parts of the desert can be covered in desert flowers. They have grown from seeds that may have been lying there for many years. These seeds grow into plants when there is just the right amount of rain at the right time of year.

Flowers make a sweet juice called NECTAR.

POLLEN is a yellow powder.

POLLINATION happens when a grain of pollen from a stamen lands on the stigma of another flower like itself.

STIGMA

STAMEN

Desert flowers bloom for just a short time. Insects drink nectar from them. Pollination happens when insects spread pollen from one flower to another. This process allows the flowers to make new seeds that drop to the ground. Those seeds will grow and flower another time.

HONEYPOT
ANT

PINACATE
(pin a COT ee)
BEETLE, also called a
STINK BEETLE

Night is the time when most insects, birds and other animals become active in the desert. The starlit sky is clear and the air is cooler. The creatures begin to move about. A honeypot ant stores nectar in its body. A pinacate beetle creeps around the desert floor.

GOLDEN WHEEL SPIDER

SCORPION

STINGER

A golden wheel spider folds up its legs and then can cartwheel down a sand dune to escape anything that bothers it. A scorpion is busy hunting for insects and other small animals in the sand. It kills its food with a poisonous stinger in its tail.

Lizards and snakes move along the desert floor. The gecko lizard flicks its sticky tongue to catch insects. The fringe-toed lizard can dig itself into the sand for protection within seconds to escape enemies. The horned lizard is covered with sharp points for protection. The Gila monster is a big poisonous lizard.

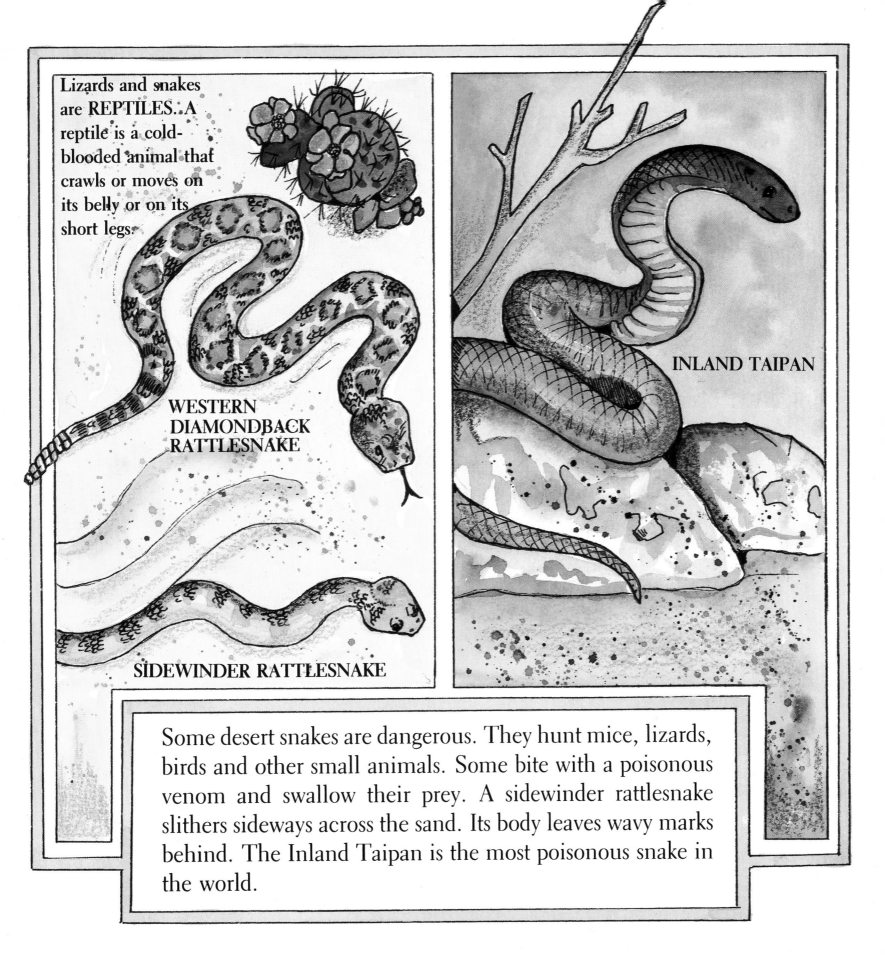

Lizards and snakes are REPTILES. A reptile is a cold-blooded animal that crawls or moves on its belly or on its short legs.

WESTERN DIAMONDBACK RATTLESNAKE

SIDEWINDER RATTLESNAKE

INLAND TAIPAN

Some desert snakes are dangerous. They hunt mice, lizards, birds and other small animals. Some bite with a poisonous venom and swallow their prey. A sidewinder rattlesnake slithers sideways across the sand. Its body leaves wavy marks behind. The Inland Taipan is the most poisonous snake in the world.

HAWK

GILA WOODPECKERS

Some desert birds live in cactus plants. Sometimes pairs of Gila woodpeckers nest inside a tall saguaro cactus. When they abandon the nest other birds such as the elf owl moves in. Vultures are very big desert birds. They live off dead animals. They are scavengers and help keep the desert clean.

TURKEY VULTURE

ELF OWL

ROADRUNNER

The roadrunner is a very fast desert bird. It runs quickly to catch insects, lizards and snakes. It hardly ever flies. The roadrunner can run as fast as twenty-three miles an hour.

Other desert creatures move about. A kangaroo rat is a small animal that is about a foot long. It can jump ten feet at a time. It eats mostly seeds. A jackrabbit doesn't need to drink much water. It gets most of its water from the plants it eats. A jackrabbit can leap fifteen feet at a time!

Desert creatures have to watch out for coyotes. They look a lot like a dog with a bushy tail. Coyotes bark, howl and whimper to communicate with other coyotes. At night a coyote's howl sounds lonely.

BOBCAT

STRIPED
SKUNK

BADGER

HARRIS
ANTELOPE
GROUND SQUIRREL

Desert skunks eat almost anything. Many deserts are home for badgers, ground squirrels, bobcats and many other animals. Most of them are small. There isn't enough food and water in the desert for large wild animals to survive.

An OASIS is a place in the desert where there are trees, plants, and water.

Some people live in deserts. Often they live in groups called tribes. Some tribes are nomadic. This means they move from one place to another, often carrying and trading goods. They may travel from oasis to oasis.

EYELIDS
EYELASHES
NOSTRILS
CAMEL

Desert people live in harsh conditions. Some wear special clothing to protect them from the sun and sand. Some use camels to get around. Their wide feet allow them to walk over soft desert sand without sinking in. Long eyelashes and thin eyelids, which they can see through when closed, keep sand out of their eyes. They can shut their nostrils to keep sand out, too.

A DROMEDARY CAMEL has one hump, and is native to Arabian deserts.

— HUMP

A BACTRIAN CAMEL has two humps, and is native to Central Asia.

Camels can go for days without water and food while traveling across the desert sands. Some scientists believe camels live off the fat stored in their humps on their backs. They can carry heavy loads, up to a thousand pounds!

SODIUM NITRATE
is used in
fertilizer.

Many natural resources have been found under desert floors. Oil, natural gas, nickel and sodium nitrate have been found under the Arabian, Sahara, American and Australian deserts. Gold and diamonds also have been found under deserts.

Deserts have some of the most interesting landscapes in the world. These hot, rocky and sandy places are home to many plants and animals. Deserts are alive with mystery and beauty.

DESERTS...DESERTS...DESERTS...

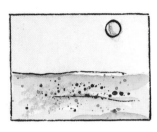

The Atacama desert in northern Chile is the driest desert in the world. Parts of that desert have had no rain in 400 years.

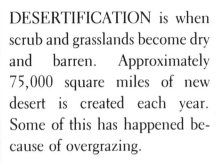

The hottest temperature ever measured in the shade was 136 degrees Fahrenheit (58 degrees Celsius) in the Sahara desert in 1922.

The Sahara desert in North Africa is about the size of the entire United States.

DESERTIFICATION is when scrub and grasslands become dry and barren. Approximately 75,000 square miles of new desert is created each year. Some of this has happened because of overgrazing.

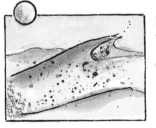

Some sandstorms can be so powerful that they can whip up sand as high as 10,000 feet.

Some deserts are very cold. The Earth's polar regions are called cold deserts where any moisture quickly freezes.

Sand dunes move. The wind blows sand up one side of a dune and it slips down the other side. Dunes can move as much as 150 feet a year.

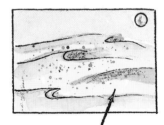

Sand dunes in the Sahara desert can be as high as 1000 feet and can stretch for miles.

Many desert buildings, called adobes, are built from mud bricks.

African Bushmen living in the Kalahari desert oil their bodies. Then the desert dust covers their skin to protect them from the sun.